Smithsonian

LITTLE EXPLORER

POWERFUL PRAYING MANTIDS

by Melissa Higgins

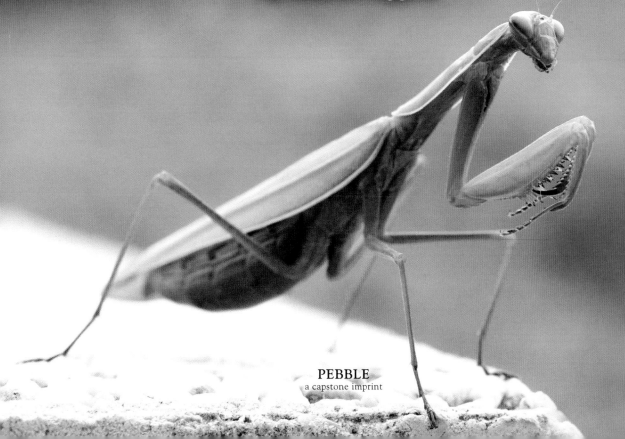

PEBBLE
a capstone imprint

Little Explorer is published by Pebble, an imprint of Capstone.
1710 Roe Crest Drive
North Mankato, Minnesota 56003
www.capstonepub.com

The name of the Smithsonian Institution and the sunburst
logo are registered trademarks of the Smithsonian Institution.
For more information, please visit www.si.edu.

Library of Congress Cataloging-in-Publication Data is available
on the Library of Congress website.

ISBN: 978-1-9771-1433-4 (library binding)
ISBN: 978-1-9771-1790-8 (paperback)
ISBN: 978-1-9771-1437-2 (eBook PDF)

Summary: Young readers are introduced to the amazing variety
of praying mantids from around the world while learning about
their behavior, life cycle, and more.

Image Credits
Alamy: age fotostock, 11 (bottom), Bryan Reynolds, 23, Tim
Gainey, 17; iStockphoto: Kaan Sezer, 7 (top), Vince Adam, 9;
Shutterstock: Bankim Desai, 7 (middle), Cathy Keifer, 5 (top),
7 (bottom right), 25 (bottom), 29, Chechu de la Fuente, 11 (top),
Dave Welch, 13, Eric Isselee, 5 (bottom), 19 (bottom), IamTK, 27,
kunchit jantana, 2, Marek R. Swadzba, 7 (bottom left), Melinda
Fawver, 25 (middle), Mr. SUTTIPON YAKHAM, 25 (top),
Ondrej Prosicky, 21, Patricia Chumillas, 12, Sebastian Janicki,
cover, Stubblefield Photography, 15, YSK1, 26, Yzoa, 1, Zaruba
Ondrej, 19 (top)

Editorial Credits
Editor: Abby Huff; Designer: Kyle Grenz; Media Researcher:
Tracy Cummins; Production Specialist: Katy LaVigne

Our very special thanks to Gary Hevel, Public Information
Officer (Emeritus), Entomology Department, at the Smithsonian
National Museum of Natural History. Capstone would also like
to thank Kealy Gordon, Product Development Manager, and the
following at Smithsonian Enterprises: Ellen Nanney, Licensing
Manager; Brigid Ferraro, Vice President, Education and Consumer
Products; and Carol LeBlanc, Senior Vice President, Education
and Consumer Products.

All internet sites appearing in back matter were available and
accurate when this book was sent to press.

Table of Contents

Words in **bold** are in the glossary.

Gentle or Fierce?

The praying mantid has a gentle name. But this insect is fierce. Its folded front legs quickly snatch **prey**. The legs have long spikes. The spikes hold the mantid's meal and don't let it slip away.

Mantids use **camouflage**. The colors and shape of their bodies blend in with where they live. Mantids hide from enemies and surprise prey.

There are about 2,000 known **species** of praying mantids. Most live in warm places.

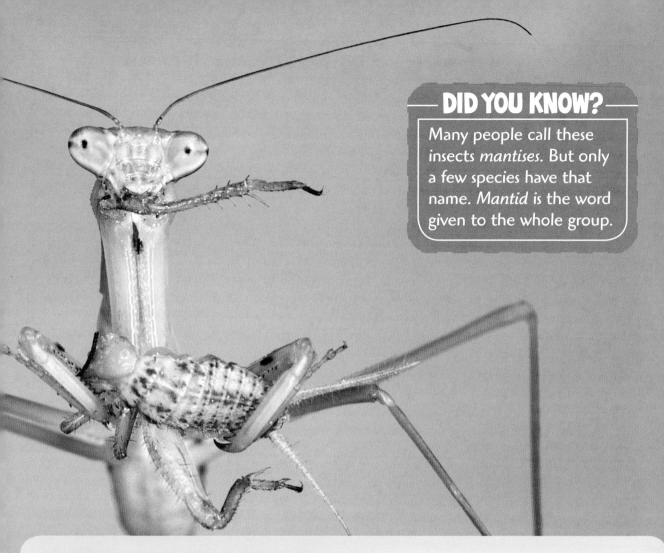

DID YOU KNOW?

Many people call these insects *mantises*. But only a few species have that name. *Mantid* is the word given to the whole group.

A Mantid's Body

Praying mantids are insects. They have six legs and three body parts. They also have two sets of wings. You can tell a mantid by its long body and bent front legs. Two big eyes give it good vision for hunting.

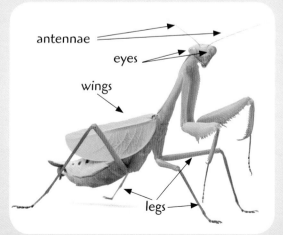

antennae

eyes

wings

legs

5

Spiny Flower Mantids

Found: Africa
Length: 1 to 1.5 inches (2.5 to 3.8 centimeters)

Spiny flower mantids are masters of **disguise**. Two large spots dot each wing. **Predators** think the spots are the eyes of a bigger animal. They leave the mantid alone.

Baby spiny flower mantids have a disguise of their own. They look like ants. Their bodies change as they grow. Later, they blend in with flowers or leaves. This keeps them hidden until they grow wings. Then they can fly from danger.

- DID YOU KNOW? -
Many animals eat mantids, including birds, bats, and snakes.

A Praying Mantid's Life

Female mantids lay up to 400 eggs in a watery froth. The froth dries into a hard case. It helps keep the eggs safe. Eggs hatch baby mantids called **nymphs**. They look like tiny adults without wings. Nymphs **molt** as they grow into adults. Most live less than one year.

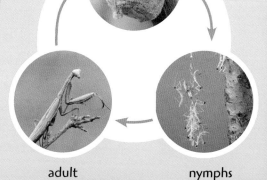

egg case

adult

nymphs

Orchid Mantids

Found: Southeast Asia
Length: 1 to 2.75 inches (2.5 to 7 cm)

A young orchid mantid looks like a flower. Its shape and color hide it from enemies. But its body also draws in insects. A fly, bee, or moth sees the mantid. The bug thinks the mantid's pink legs are flower petals. The bug flies close to check it out. Then the mantid grabs the bug. It eats its meal.

DID YOU KNOW?

Mantids are meat eaters. They feed on insects such as flies, crickets, and grasshoppers. Big mantids can eat lizards, frogs, snakes, birds, and rodents.

Mediterranean Mantids

Found: Europe, North America, and Western Asia
Length: Up to 2.5 inches (6.5 cm)

A bird hunts for dinner. It spies a Mediterranean mantid. This mantid does not run. It faces its enemy. It lifts its front legs and raises its wings. The wings have two spots. They look like big eyes. The mantid has another trick to scare away animals. It rubs its hind wings together. They make a loud scraping noise.

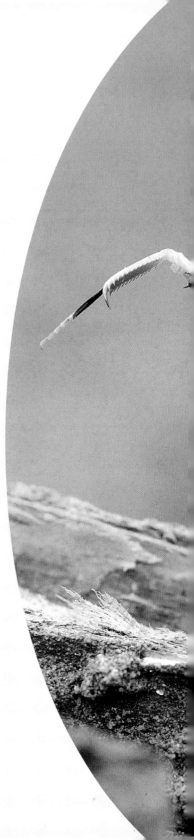

DID YOU KNOW?

Praying mantids might look scary, but they are harmless to people. They do not sting or use **venom**.

Looking at You

All mantids can turn their heads 180 degrees. That's a half circle. They are the only insects that can turn their head so far. This helps them spot food and foes.

Giant Asian Mantids

Found: Southeast Asia
Length: 3 to 3.5 inches (7.6 to 9 cm)

The giant Asian mantid is big!
It's the size of a human palm. Most
mantids wait for food to come to
them. Giant Asian mantids hunt.
They chase animals up to half
their size. Like all mantids, they
use **mandibles** to eat. The sharp
mouthparts chew and tear.

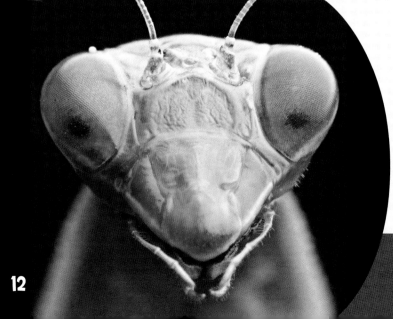

All mantids
have mandibles.

Giant Asian mantids are green, yellow, or brown. They can change color to blend in with their home. Changing color takes a few days.

DID YOU KNOW?

Mantids eat other mantids. Females sometimes eat males after they **mate**. A baby mantid's first meal is often one of its brothers or sisters.

Chinese Mantids

Found: Asia, Europe, and North America
Length: 2 to 5 inches (5.1 to 12.7 cm)

The Chinese mantid is from Asia. In the late 1800s, some came to the United States on plants from China. People also bought them. They put the mantids in gardens to eat bad bugs. Now Chinese mantids live across North America and Europe. They are known as an **invasive species**. They spread in ways that are harmful to native plants and animals.

Good or Bad for Gardens?

Some gardeners like praying mantids. They eat insect pests, such as **aphids**. But there is a downside to mantids. They also eat bugs that are good for plants, such as moths and butterflies. These insects spread pollen. Plants need pollen to make new plants.

Chinese mantids go after big prey. They even eat hummingbirds. At least 12 kinds of praying mantids eat small birds.

Grass Mantids

Found: North America, South America, and Southeast Asia
Length: 2.2 to 2.75 inches (5.5 to 7 cm)

Is that a blade of grass? Look closer. It is a grass mantid. Green ones are found in living grass. They blend in. Brown grass mantids live in dry grass and pine needles.

Most mantids mate to make eggs. Some grass mantids are different. The female can make eggs by herself. This is a way some animals have **adapted**. They can survive even if no males are around.

The Indian grass mantid has a very thin body.

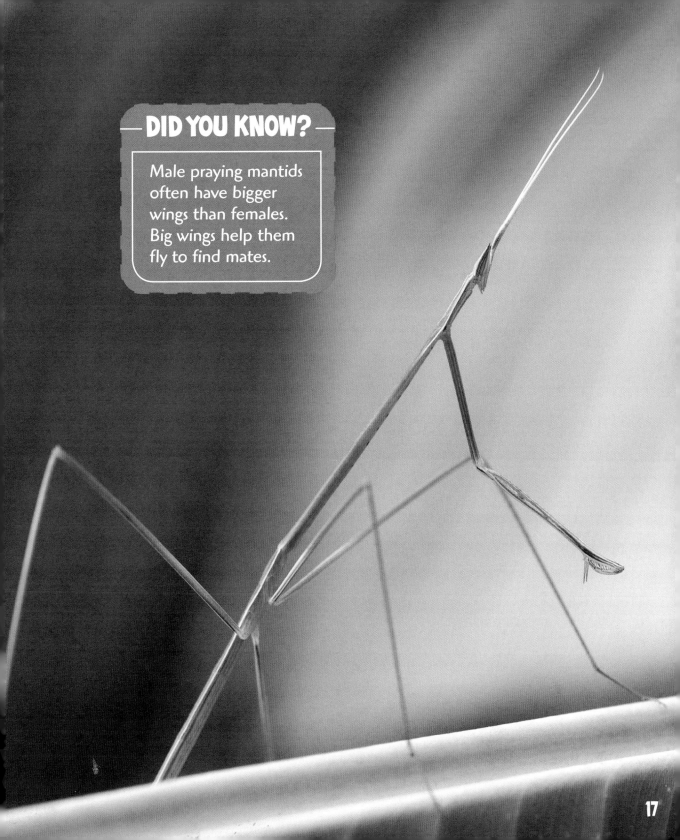

DID YOU KNOW?

Male praying mantids often have bigger wings than females. Big wings help them fly to find mates.

Dead Leaf Mantids

Found: Africa, South America, and Southeast Asia
Length: 1.8 to 3.3 inches (4.5 to 8.5 cm)

It's easy to see how the dead leaf mantid got its name. Its brown colors are the same as old leaves. The edges of its body are bumpy. They look like tiny rips.

One type of dead leaf mantid hangs from a twig. If touched, it sways like a leaf in a breeze. If touched too hard, it drops to the ground. Then watch your step! These mantids blend in with the forest floor.

DID YOU KNOW?

At least two styles of martial arts are based on the movements of praying mantids.

Batty

Most praying mantids have just one ear. It's found under the belly. It does not hear the sounds human ears do. It hears high-pitched sounds made by bats as they hunt. A mantid's ear warns it to get away from the bat.

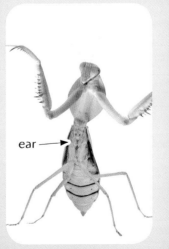

ear

Shield Mantids

Found: Central and South America
Length: About 3.5 inches (9 cm)

This green mantid has a large flap behind its head. People say it looks like a shield.

The shield mantid's green body also looks like a leaf. It matches the plants where it lives. This disguise fools prey and predators. Small birds that do spot the shield mantid might not eat it. The mantid's flaps are very wide. They are hard to swallow.

DID YOU KNOW?

Mantids strike fast! They grab prey six times faster than people can blink their eyes.

Shield mantids are also called leaf mantids and hooded mantids.

Ground Mantids

Found: North America and Australia
Length: 0.4 to 1.2 inches (1 to 3 cm)

The ground mantid does not wait for prey. It chases food. This small mantid lives on the ground. Its brown body blends in with sand and dirt.

The ground mantid quickly runs from danger. It hides under plants. It also protects itself by standing tall and sticking out its arms. This is meant to scare off predators.

Skinner's ground mantid

Stick Mantids

Found: Africa, Asia, Australia, North America,
and South America
Length: 2.8 to 6 inches (7 to 15 cm)

Most mantids live in shrubs and trees. So looking like a stick is a good disguise. Some stick mantids are thin. They look like small twigs. Others are thick. They look like bumpy wood.

Stick mantids can be very big. The giant African stick mantid grows up to 6 inches (15.2 cm) long. It sits still. It waits for prey to come close enough to grab.

DID YOU KNOW?

Praying mantids eat their prey head-first.

The African twig mantid holds out its front legs to look more like a stick.

Praying Mantid or Walking Stick Insect?

It's easy to mistake praying mantids for walking stick insects. Both are long. They blend in with their **habitats**. How can you tell them apart? Most walking sticks have thin heads. Their front legs do not fold up. Praying mantids only eat animals. Walking sticks only eat plants.

praying mantid

walking stick insect

Bark Mantids

Found: Central and West Africa, Australia, and
      Southeast Asia
Length: 0.78 to 1.6 inches (2 to 4 cm)

The bark mantid sits on a tree trunk.
It has brown, gray, and olive stripes.
These colors match the tree bark.
The mantid also presses its flat body
against the tree. Predators have a
hard time seeing it.

DID YOU KNOW?

Baby bark mantids look like black ants. Many other young mantids do too. Birds don't like how ants taste. They often leave the young mantids alone.

Most female mantids leave their eggs after laying them. One kind of female bark mantid stays with her eggs. She keeps them safe from wasps, ants, and beetles.

Unicorn Mantids

Found: Southeast Asia, North America, and
     South America
Length: 2 to 3.5 inches (5 to 9 cm)

This mantid has a spike on its head. People think it looks like a unicorn's horn. Scientists are not sure why the mantid has the spike. It looks a bit like a leaf bud or a thorn. The spike might help the mantid blend in with plants.

Some young unicorn mantids use another disguise. They curl the back part of their bodies. It looks like a **scorpion's** tail. Predators stay away.

Texas unicorn mantid

A unicorn mantid really has two spikes. They come close together as the mantid grows.

Glossary

adapt (uh-DAPT)—to change in order to survive

aphid (AY-fid)—an insect that sucks plant juices

camouflage (KA-muh-flahzh)—an animal's coloring or shape that helps it blend in with things around it

disguise (dis-GAHYZ)—an animal's coloring or shape that makes it look like something else

habitat (HAB-uh-tat)—the natural place or type of place in which a plant or animal lives

invasive species (in-VAY-siv SPEE-seez)—a plant or animal that has been brought into a place it is not naturally found and is spreading in a way that harms native plants or animals

mandibles (MAN-duh-buhlz)—strong mouthparts used to chew

mate (MATE)—to join together and produce young

molt (MOLT)—to shed an outer layer of skin

nymph (NIMF)—a young form of an insect

predator (PRED-uh-tur)—an animal that hunts other animals for food

prey (PRAY)—an animal hunted by another animal for food

scorpion (SKAWR-pee-uhn)—an animal with a curved tail that has a stinger at the end

species (SPEE-seez)—a group of living things that can reproduce with one another

venom (VEN-uhm)—a poisonous liquid made by some animals

Critical Thinking Questions

1. Praying mantids are hunters. What about their bodies make them good at catching prey?

2. If bug pests were in your garden, would you bring in mantids to help deal with the problem? Why or why not?

3. Pick one praying mantid from this book. How is it different from other mantids?

Read More

Amstutz, Lisa J. *Praying Mantises*. North Mankato, MN: Capstone Press, 2018.

Martins, Dino. *You Can Be an Entomologist!* Washington, D.C.: National Geographic, 2019.

Orr, Tamra B. *Praying Mantis*. Ann Arbor, MI: Cherry Lake Publishing, 2016.

Internet Sites

National Geographic Kids: Praying Mantis
https://kids.nationalgeographic.com/animals/invertebrates/insects/praying-mantis/

Switch Zoo: Praying Mantis
https://switchzoo.com/profiles/prayingmantis.htm

Index